INSIDE THE SITUATION ROOM

HOW A PHOTOGRAPH SHOWED AMERICA DEFEATING OSAMA BIN LADEN

by Dan Elish

Content Adviser: Dennis Showalter, PhD,
Professor of History
Colorado College

COMPASS POINT BOOKS
a capstone imprint

Compass Point Books are published by Capstone Press,
1710 Roe Crest Drive, North Mankato, Minnesota 56003
www.mycapstone.com

Editorial Credits
Michelle Bisson, editor; Tracy McCabe, designer; Svetlana Zhurkin, media researcher;
Kathy McColley, production specialist; Kathleen Baxter, library consultant

Content Adviser: Dennis Showalter, PhD, Professor of History, Colorado College

Photo Credits
Courtesy of the Federal Bureau of Investigations, 27, 57 (left); Getty Images: Ethan
Miller, 33; Newscom: Abaca USA/Douliery Olivier, 39, Abaca/Balkis Press, 23, MCT/
Levings, 16, Polaris, 25, 56, Reuters/Faisal Mahmood, 7, Reuters/Kamil Krzaczynski,
52, Reuters/Kevin Lamarque, 53, Reuters/Khalil Ashawi, 51, Reuters/Russell Boyce,
5, Sipa/Haley, 48, Sipa/Makouka, 46; Official White House Photo by Chuck Kennedy,
10, 58 (bottom left); Official White House Photo by Pete Souza, cover, 6, 17, 31, 40,
41, 58 (bottom right); Shutterstock: Dan Howell, 57 (right), getideaka, 21, JStone,
55, Orlok, 45, 50, 59 (bottom); U.S. Air Force: Tech. Sgt. Gregory Brook, 8, 14; U.S.
Navy: Ensign Danny Ewing Jr., 13, Mass Communication Specialist 3rd Class Geneva
G. Brier, 42, Paul Farley, 19, Photographer's Mate 1st Class Arlo K. Abrahamson,
28, 58 (top), Photographer's Mate 3rd Class John DeCoursey, 37; Wikimedia/U.S.
Department of Defense, 35, 59 (top).

Library of Congress Cataloging-in-Publication Data
Names: Elish, Dan, author. Title: Inside the situation room : how a photograph showed
America defeating Osama bin Laden / by Dan Elish. Description: North Mankato,
Minnesota : Compass Point Books, 2019. | Audience: 8-10. | Audience: 4-8. Identifiers:
LCCN 2018018480 (print) | LCCN 2018031678 (ebook) | ISBN 9780756558833
(eBook PDF) | ISBN 9780756558796 | ISBN 9780756558796?(hardcover) | ISBN
9780756558819?(pbk.) Subjects: LCSH: Bin Laden, Osama, 1957-2011--Assassination-
-Juvenile literature. | Bin Laden, Osama, 1957-2011--Juvenile literature. | United
States. Navy. SEALs--History--21st century--Juvenile literature. | Special operations
(Military science)--United States--Juvenile literature. | Special operations (Military
science)--Pakistan--Juvenile literature. | Terrorism--United States--Prevention--Juvenile
literature. | War on Terrorism, 2001-2009--Juvenile literature. | Middle East--Politics and
government--21st century--Juvenile literature. Classification: LCC HV6430.B55 (ebook) |
LCC HV6430.B55 E45 2019 (print) | DDC 958.104/6092 [B] --dc23 LC record available at
https://lccn.loc.gov/2018018480

Printed in the United States of America
1798

TABLEOFCONTENTS

ChapterOne: SEAL Team Six.................................... 4

ChapterTwo: Who Was Osama bin Laden?............. 20

ChapterThree: The Long Wait 30

ChapterFour: The Middle East After bin Laden...... 44

Timeline 56

Glossary 60

Additional Resources 61

Source Notes 62

Select Bibliography 63

Index 64

ChapterOne
SEAL TEAM SIX

The U.S. had sought to capture Osama bin Laden for more than a decade. The leader of the terrorist organization al-Qaida, bin Laden was the mastermind behind the attacks on New York City's World Trade Center and Washington D.C.'s Pentagon on September 11, 2001—attacks that took almost 3,000 lives. As early as 1998 President Bill Clinton had tried—but failed—to kill bin Laden with cruise missiles. In late 2001 President George W. Bush had gone to war in Afghanistan to root out al-Qaida and bring bin Laden to justice, dead or alive.

Still, bin Laden remained at large. Worse, when Barack Obama was sworn in as president on January 20, 2009, the trail had gone cold. U.S. intelligence had no concrete leads as to bin Laden's whereabouts. Though some in the U.S. government were ready to give up the hunt, the new president made it his top priority to bring bin Laden to justice for his crimes against humanity. Early in his term, on May 26, 2009, he concluded a routine meeting on national security by pointing at Thomas Donilon, the deputy national security adviser; Leon Panetta, the newly appointed CIA director; Mike Leiter, the director of the National Counterterrorism Center; and Rahm Emanuel, White House chief of staff.

This is an example of one of the many posters created in the hunt for Osama bin Laden.

"You, you, you, and you," the president said. "Come upstairs."

Once they were gathered together, Obama laid out the mission for his team. "Here's the deal," he said. "I want this hunt for Osama bin Laden . . . to come to the front of the line. . . . This has to be our top priority and it needs leadership in the tops of your organizations. . . . I want regular reports on this to me and I want them starting in 30 days."

Obama and his chief advisers met in the Situation Room to decide what to do about bin Laden.

It took two solid years of searching, but the CIA and U.S. National Geospatial Agency finally located a compound in Pakistan using its ultrasophisticated technology. They thought bin Laden was hiding there in a three-story home behind stone walls. Every day a tall man who fit bin Laden's description walked in the backyard of the compound. Was this "pacer," as he was called, the international terrorist? Even with modern tracking equipment and satellite imagery, the CIA could not be 100 percent certain. After hours of discussion at the highest levels of government, President Obama made his decision. The likelihood that the pacer was bin Laden was high enough to warrant an attack. The U.S. was finally going to get its enemy.

This is what bin Laden's compound looked like from the outside.

After hours of discussion, they were left with three main options. First, U.S. warplanes could bomb the compound. But that would mean sending warplanes into Pakistan. Though the nation was suspected of having terrorist ties, it also sometimes acted as an ally of the United States. To makes matters worse, bin Laden's compound was located near a Pakistani military base. What if the Pakistani soldiers became alerted to the bombing raid and fired at the U.S. planes? The last thing Obama wanted was to start a battle with an ally. On top of that, Obama and his team realized that a powerful, destructive blast would make it almost impossible to identify bin Laden's body. If Obama were going to risk sending

U.S. troops into Pakistan to kill the world's most notorious terrorist, he would need proof that he had gotten his man.

Option two involved using a drone strike to take out bin Laden on one of his morning walks. Again, while this strategy had the advantage of keeping U.S. troops out of harm's way, if successful, it would also make it impossible to say for sure if the pacer truly was bin Laden or not.

Finally, there was option three. The U.S. could

With boots on the ground, Obama would know for certain whether U.S. forces had gotten the job done.

send in a highly trained team of Navy SEALs. SEALs stands for SEa, Air, and Land—the three areas of the special force's operations. To send in the SEALs and complete the mission successfully would be difficult. Helicopters would have to fly under Pakistani radar and execute a difficult landing at the compound. Then the team would have to blast its way to the third floor of the house where bin Laden was thought to be hiding. The risks were great, but the benefits were even greater. With boots on the ground, Obama would know for certain whether U.S. forces had gotten the job done. At the same time, Navy SEALs could scour the compound for computers, papers, and any other materials that might provide clues to future al-Qaida operations.

Obama picked option three. The man chosen to lead and train the elite group of Navy SEALs was one of the country's experts in special operations, Admiral William H. McRaven. On the night of May 1, 2011, 24 members of Navy SEAL Team Six were stationed just across the Pakistani border in Jalalabad, Afghanistan. They were poised and ready to strike. On Saturday afternoon, Obama placed a call to McRaven. "Godspeed to you and your forces," the president said. "Please pass on to them my personal thanks for their service." Then he added, "I will personally be following this mission very closely."

President Barack Obama and his wife, Michelle, stand backstage at the White House Correspondents' Dinner before his speech.

Indeed he would. But first, the duties of the presidency called. The White House Correspondents' Dinner, an annual event for journalists who cover the White House, was to take place the night before the raid. The annual dinner features a big-name comedian who generally roasts the sitting president, but that president is also expected to give a comic speech. After giving the go-ahead for the operation, Obama could have opted out of the dinner, but the president and his advisers thought it essential to give no clues whatsoever that anything unusual was in the works. The last thing they wanted was for bin Laden to learn that his location had been compromised. So Obama attended the correspondents' dinner and delivered a comedy routine.

The next morning, in an effort to keep what was brewing hidden from the press, Obama stuck to his normal routine and played golf.

Meanwhile, halfway around the world in Afghanistan, it was late afternoon. McRaven had planned the attack for one o'clock in the morning when, with any luck, the compound would be quiet and everyone inside asleep. This meant that the mission would launch at 2:30 p.m. Eastern time. Panetta had official command from a conference room at the CIA headquarters in Langley, Virginia, while McRaven was at his post in Jalalabad. At the same time, a satellite would send a video feed of the operation in real time to the White House. The final order to start the operation came from Panetta: "Go in there and get bin Laden."

Two Stealth Blackhawk helicopters took off from Afghanistan at approximately 11:15 p.m. local time. Each SEAL was fully equipped with desert camouflage, helmet, night-vision goggles, and various weapons, including automatic rifles outfitted with silencers. About 10 minutes into the flight, as the choppers crossed into Pakistani airspace, three larger helicopters called Chinooks took off from Afghanistan and settled in various parts of Pakistan. They were on duty to give support in case the Pakistani military discovered the raid and started a firefight.

With skillful piloting, the two Stealth helicopters made it past the Pakistani military base to the compound. The plan called for one helicopter to drop the SEAL team onto the compound roof by ropes. Instead, the first chopper clipped the top of the compound wall. Later, it was discovered that the air at the compound was too thin to allow the helicopter to fly. Unable to stay airborne unless it kept moving, the chopper began to lose altitude. Disaster was looming. If the Blackhawk flipped to its side, its rotors would dig into the ground, causing fatalities to the crew and a possible explosion. Luckily, the pilot was able to perform a daring controlled crash, planting the helicopter's nose in the dirt.

Stealth Blackhawk helicopters are designed for difficult missions.

Inside the White House, the president's chief advisers were watching the action on a video feed. Though some advisers felt that the president shouldn't watch the raid in real time, Obama walked into the room, saying, "I need to watch this."

So the scene was set for one of the most famous images of the Obama presidency. Secretary of State Hillary Clinton walked into the room behind Obama. That's when White House photographer Pete Souza

Navy SEALs train rigorously for their difficult missions.

snapped a photo of Obama and his team, stone silent, anxiously waiting to see how the mission would turn out. Obama later said that the moments waiting to see what happened after the chopper went down were among the longest in his life.

Thankfully, back in Jalalabad, McRaven soon made sure that everyone in the chopper was safe.

"Mr. Director," McRaven told Panetta, "As you can see, we have a helicopter down in the courtyard. My men are prepared for this . . . and will deal with it."

Indeed, one of the reasons Obama had picked the Navy SEALs for the job was their ability to improvise in the field. Moving quickly along the inside wall of the compound, the SEALs blew open a door that led into the house. On the first floor, they shot and killed Abrar Ahmed, one of bin Laden's couriers, and Ahmed's wife, Bushra. When they encountered a steel door leading to a stairway, they blew it open with a C-4 explosive. On the second floor, they killed bin Laden's son Khalid. On the third floor, the SEALs tackled two of bin Laden's wives, then saw a tall, bearded man in a prayer cap. When the man retreated to a bedroom, the SEALs followed, believing they recognized him as bin Laden. He was hiding behind two more of his wives. The SEALs shot him twice in the head. After years of searching, the SEALs had killed Osama bin Laden, the world's most dangerous terrorist.

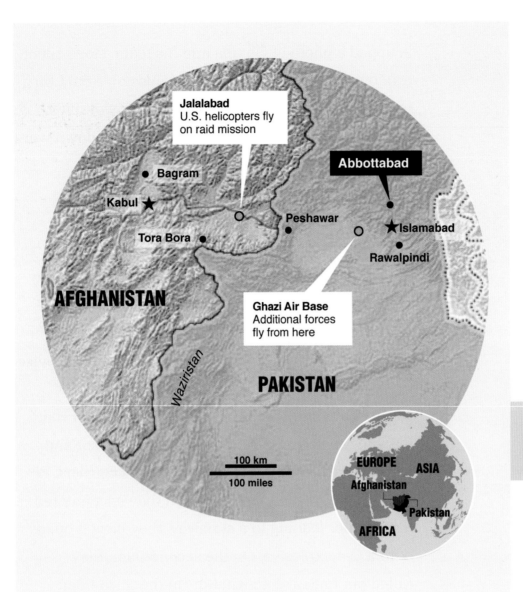

Jalalabad
U.S. helicopters fly
on raid mission

Abbottabad

● Bagram

Kabul ★

Tora Bora ●

Peshawar ●

★Islamabad

Rawalpindi ●

AFGHANISTAN

Waziristan

Ghazi Air Base
Additional forces
fly from here

PAKISTAN

100 km
100 miles

EUROPE   ASIA
Afghanistan
Pakistan
AFRICA

This map shows
the SEAL Team
Six mission.

McRaven heard the news first. "For God and
Country," a SEAL reported. "Geronimo . . . E.K.I.A,"
for "enemy killed in action." This meant that
bin Laden had been killed. At the White House,
Obama heard this and said, "We got him." Still,
before announcing the news to the world, the
president wanted to make absolutely sure. After a

THE ROOM WHERE IT HAPPENED

President Obama and his team, including Vice President Joe Biden (left) and Hillary Clinton wait anxiously to hear whether the mission had succeeded.

Many moments in U.S. history are remembered through one special photograph, an image that captures the spirit of the time. The 1851 painting of George Washington crossing the Delaware River by German American artist Emanuael Gottlieb Leutze became a symbol of the colonists' fight for freedom in the Revolutionary War (1775-1783). The photograph of five marines raising the U.S. flag on the Pacific Island of Iwo Jima shows the struggle of World War II (1939-1945). And the image of President Obama and his team anxiously waiting to hear news of the U.S. raid on bin Laden's compound perfectly captures the tension of a particular night in history and the entire post–9/11 era.

The people in the room, starting from the left side of the table and working clockwise:

Joe Biden, vice president

Barack Obama, president

Brig. Gen. Marshall B. Webb (seated at the head of the table, with a laptop), assistant commanding general of the Joint Special Operations Command

Admiral Michael Mullen (standing, wearing a tie), chairman of the Joint Chiefs of Staff and principal military adviser to the president

Thomas E. Donilon (standing, arms folded), President Obama's national security adviser

Bill Daley (standing, with jacket), White House Chief of Staff for President Obama from January 2011 to 2012.

Denis McDonough (seated), deputy national security adviser

Tony Blinken (standing, peering over Daley's shoulder), national security adviser to the vice president

Hillary Rodham Clinton, secretary of state

Audrey Tomason (standing, farthest in back), a director for counterterrorism

John O. Brennan (standing, wearing gray), assistant to Obama for counterterrorism

James R. Clapper Jr. (standing, wearing tie), director of National Intelligence

Robert M. Gates (seated), secretary of defense

facial identification was made, bin Laden's body was flown back to Afghanistan. McRaven asked the troops on the ground how tall the body was. The answer: between 6' 4" and 6' 5" (1.93 and 1.96 m), which was bin Laden's height. Still, McRaven also wanted to be sure. When the commanding officer couldn't find a tape measure, he asked a SEAL who was 6' (1.83 m) tall to lie down next to the body. The body was about 4 inches (10 cm) longer than the SEAL.

McRaven called the president.

"Mr. President, I have fairly high confidence that we have killed bin Laden here," he said.

DNA evidence would later confirm that the man they'd killed was bin Laden, but President Obama and his team were satisfied now.

That night at 11:35 p.m. Eastern time, Obama went on national TV to make the announcement: "Good evening. Tonight I can report to the American people and to the world that the United States has conducted an operation that killed Osama bin laden, the leader of al-Qaida and a terrorist who's responsible for the murder of thousands of innocent men, women, and children."

A DOG CALLED CAIRO

SEAL Team Six dogs often become pets when they retire from the service.

President Obama was surprised to learn that SEAL Team Six traveled with a dog named Cairo. When the president traveled to Fort Campbell, Kentucky, to congratulate the SEALs five days after killing bin Laden, Obama said, "I want to meet that dog."

The squadron commander of the Navy SEAL team joked, "If you want to meet the dog, Mr. President, I advise you to bring treats." Obama did head over to pet the dog. But the animal's muzzle was kept on as part of standard procedure.

ChapterTwo
WHO WAS OSAMA BIN LADEN?

On March 10, 1957, Saudi Arabian construction billionaire Mohammed bin Awad bin Laden and his wife, Syrian-born Alia Ghanoum, welcomed a son, Osama bin Laden, into their family. The seventh of 60 children born to Mohammad bin Laden, Osama was the only child from his father's marriage to Alia. However, Osama barely got to know his father before his parents divorced. He spent the bulk of his childhood with his mother, her new husband, and four stepsiblings. The elder bin Laden died in a plane crash in 1967, when Osama was 10.

Young Osama was a shy, but brilliant student. At 14, he was invited to join a highly regarded study group whose goal was to memorize the entire Koran. The teacher of the group was the first to expose him to a pure form of Islam that called for living by a literal interpretation of the holy word. By their second year in school, Osama and his fellow students had become activists, preaching the faith of a pure Islamic law.

The teenage bin Laden became increasingly devout, shunning contact with women. Around age 17, he plunged into study of the written word of Egyptian scholar Sayyid Qutb, a man who, in 1966, was hanged for his beliefs. Qutb detested the

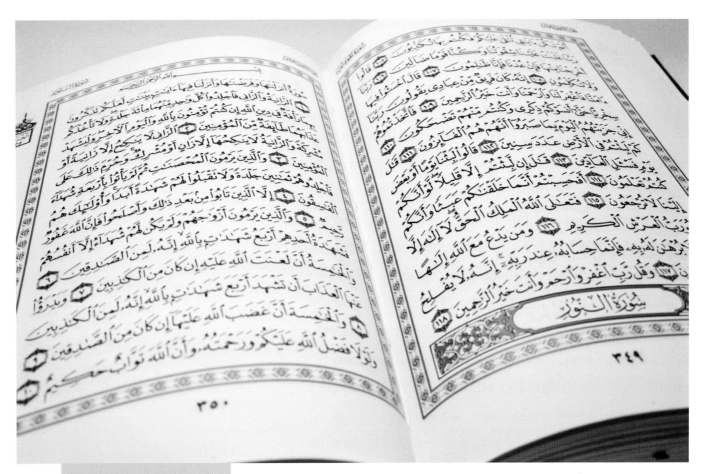

Osama bin Laden believed in a literal interpretation of the Koran.

westernization of Arab societies. A passionate anti-Semite, he argued that a pure reading of the Koran was the only true path. In his view, secular regimes were called *jahiliyya* and could be targeted for violence. Protesting the freedoms and consumerism of the West, Qutb wrote: "Islam is a system given by God and it aims to establish a fundamental principle of God's sovereignty and people's servitude to Him alone. As such, Islam has the right to remove all obstacles from its way . . ."

In other words, a pure form of Islam had the right

to use violence to remake the world in its own image. As a teen, bin Laden was already looking for ways to continue Qutb's work. In 1979 he had his chance when the Soviet Union invaded the Muslim country of Afghanistan.

At 22, no longer willing to stand back in the struggle for religious purity, bin Laden was ready to flex his muscles. He was a fighter, a man who desperately wanted to be on the front lines of the war in Afghanistan against the Soviet Union. He joined mujihadeen forces in the fight. By 1987 bin Laden had recruited his own band of about 24 Arabs, creating a small army motivated by religious purity. Equipped with weapons and bulldozers, bin Laden and his troops drove 10 miles (16 km) into Afghanistan and built an outpost near the village of Jaji. Bin Laden called his new village al-Masada or the Lion's Den. That they were stationed close to a Soviet garrison didn't bother bin Laden a bit.

He welcomed a fight with the enemy, telling a Syrian journalist: "God willing, we want the Lion's Den to be the first thing that the enemy faces. Its place as the first camp visible to the enemy means that they will focus their bombardments on us in an extreme manner."

They did so. The Soviets dropped so many bombs that the area around the Lion's Den was shorn of all vegetation. Bin Laden and his men fought valiantly.

Osama bin Laden (center) fought against the Soviets in Afghanistan.

At one point bin Laden was left unconscious, surrounded by dead soldiers. Though the battle was ultimately meaningless in terms of overall strategy, bin Laden proclaimed a stirring victory. Suddenly, he was famous for his willingness to fight. Reporters from around the Middle East flocked to see bin Laden, and he gladly gave interviews.

By the time he was 30, bin Laden was going by a new nickname, "the Sheik." He was tall and thin and wore a beard. He dressed simply. Despite his enormous personal wealth, he shunned the conveniences of modern life such as air-conditioning and fine food. In his view, God had chosen him to continue the pursuit of a pure Muslim state. In 1989 when the Soviet Union finally grew fed up with the now 10-year war in Afghanistan and retreated, bin Laden returned to Saudi Arabia as a hero. He and his men now called themselves "al-Qaida" or "the Base," the soul of a new Islamic nation.

But bin Laden would have to wait a while longer for his power to peak. In 1990 Saddam Hussein, the ruler of Iraq, invaded the small country of Kuwait. His goals were to take control of Kuwait's oil reserves, eliminate the large debt Iraq owed Kuwait, and expand Iraq's power in the region. When U.S. President George H.W. Bush sent troops to defend Kuwait, bin Laden fired off a series of letters to Saudi King Fahd. He demanded that the infidel United States not be allowed in the country, complaining that they were too close to certain holy sites. In truth, bin Laden wanted to drive the Iraqi forces from Kuwait himself in a new holy war. When the king ignored him and welcomed the U.S. soldiers, bin Laden was furious. After all, how could Saudi Arabia, the country of his birth, choose to ally itself with the United States over him? Simmering, he was expelled from Saudi Arabia, never to return, and moved back to Afghanistan.

By 1995 bin Laden and al-Qaida had been implicated in attacks on Americans and had taken

A POET AND A FIGHTER

Osama bin Laden used poetry to bring attention to the violence of al-Qaida.

Ironically, most of the money bin Laden and like-minded mujahideen groups used to fight the Russians during the Afghanistan War came from the United States. Though there were many reasons for the Russian defeat in Afghanistan, no serious scholar credits bin Laden. Still, that isn't how he saw it. In his mind, his small ragtag troupe overcame all odds to help drive the Russian infidels from the land. Bin Laden even wrote poems celebrating violence and death as a way to defend the purity of his faith. He used these gory poems as a recruiting tool to inspire young men to join the fight. One began with this image of a sword covered in blood:

He hunches forth,

Staining the blades of lances red.

responsibility for a truck bombing in Saudi Arabia that took the lives of five Americans and two Indians. Some sources say that as early as 1993 he was already talking about a giant attack on the twin towers that comprised New York's World Trade Center, in which he hoped to kill at least a quarter million people. A 1993 bombing of the World Trade Center was, however, not tied to him. In 1996 bin Laden held a press conference during which he declared war on the United States, a country that he called "the head of the snake." His demands were simple, yet outrageous: he wanted U.S. aid and troops withdrawn from Saudi Arabia and Israel. In 1998 he was even more direct, telling ABC News reporter John Miller, "I'm declaring war on the United States. I am going to attack your country."

Most Americans still hadn't heard of bin Laden. But President Bill Clinton was alarmed enough to fire cruise missiles into the compound where bin Laden was living at the time. The bomb missed bin Laden, who had left the compound an hour earlier. In 1998 al-Qaida bombed U.S. embassies in Nairobi, Kenya, and Dar es Salaam, Tanzania. In 2000 al-Qaida attacked the U.S. warship USS *Cole*. Still, most Americans and government agencies didn't take him seriously enough. After all, bin Laden wasn't even affiliated with a country. Expelled by Saudi Arabia, he was a lone actor who lived in the

"I'm declaring war on the United States. I am going to attack your country."

In 1998 al-Qaida bombed the U.S. embassy in Nairobi.

As a result of bin Laden's September 11 attacks, the U.S. invaded Iraq.

hills of Afghanistan. He had a lot of money but how could such a leader pose a threat to a country as large and militarily powerful as the United States?

On September 11, 2001, America found out. After years of planning, al-Qaida operatives hijacked four U.S. commercial jets. Two were flown into New

York's World Trade Center towers. Another was flown into the Pentagon. A fourth, likely headed for the Capitol Building in Washington, D.C., was forced by passengers to crash-land in a field in Pennsylvania. In the end, almost 3,000 people were killed. It was al-Qaida's most destructive action to date.

Undoubtedly, the 9/11 attacks had succeeded beyond bin Laden's imaginings. But they also signaled the beginning of the end for bin Laden and the severe weakening of al-Qaida. A few months later, President George W. Bush invaded Afghanistan, looking to root out al-Qaida strongholds that were protected by the Taliban government. In 2003 Bush also ordered U.S. troops into Iraq, claiming to be looking for weapons of mass destruction. It was later found that there were no such weapons.

Though many historians feel the Iraq war (2003-2011) was a mistake, Bush's maneuvers in Afghanistan successfully disrupted al-Qaida's operations. For years after 9/11, bin Laden was on the run. But by the time Bush left office in January 2009, bin Laden had disappeared. U.S. intelligence agencies had no leads. Had one of the most notorious terrorists in recent history gotten away with it? Coming into office in 2009, one of President Barack Obama's goals was to capture bin Laden. Obama would do whatever he could to get bin Laden and avenge the deaths of those killed on 9/11.

ChapterThree
THE LONG WAIT

From the beginning of the Obama presidency, White House photographer Pete Souza was given unusual access to the president and his family. As Souza put it, "I don't think there's really anyone else in the White House that has that kind of exposure to him. I mean, they may know him, the National Security team. They know him from the Situation Room, and the tense meetings in the Oval Office. But they don't see him interact with his daughters after work, or on a Saturday."

Souza, of course, had no input whatsoever on national policy. Still, by the time of the operation to take down bin Laden, he was a common fixture around the White House. "I meet Obama when he comes down from the Residence," he said, "and then I tag along with him all day until he leaves. . . . I see all the different compartments of his life. Certainly the national security adviser is in all the national security meetings. Well, so am I. . . . The point being that I'm sort of like the only person who crosses all those boundaries."

A photographer with that kind of access to the first family had the opportunity to snap many iconic photographs of the president during his eight years in office. Especially an exceptional photographer like Souza. And his ability to blend into the scenery

This photograph of Obama and the family dog, Bo, is one of many quiet moments caught by Pete Souza's camerawork.

allowed Souza to take more than just charming family pictures. He was also there when Obama and his team were waiting to hear the fate of SEAL Team Six and Osama bin Laden. As a result, he was able to take the defining picture of the Obama years, a unique photograph in U.S. history. It showed many of the highest-ranking members of the U.S. government watching, gravely concerned, as a dangerous military operation unfolded.

Some historians would argue—and Obama himself believed—that his very presidency was on the line. After all, badly executed military operations had sunk previous administrations. In 1980 a failed rescue attempt of U.S. citizens held hostage in Tehran by a group of Irani students was a major factor in President Jimmy Carter's defeat by Ronald Reagan in that year's presidential election. Obama knew that if the plan to kill bin Laden failed, he would be held responsible. Americans would take out their disappointment in the voting booth.

With so much at stake—including the lives of the Navy SEALs tasked to invade the compound —it is no wonder that Obama and his team look worried in Souza's picture. It is also understandable that in the months leading up to the raid, the major players in the photograph held varying views as to whether it should proceed at all, arguing that there wasn't enough evidence that "the pacer was bin Laden."

PETE SOUZA—PHOTOGRAPHER OF PRESIDENTS

Pete Souza traveled the country along with President Barack Obama. Here, he takes photos in a Las Vegas arena as Obama speaks about jobs and fair housing.

Pete Souza has made a career of photographing presidents. In the 1980s he was the White House photographer for Republican President Ronald Reagan, taking many pictures of Reagan and his wife, Nancy. After Reagan left the White House in 1989, Souza worked as a freelance photographer. In 2005 Souza began working for a young senator from Illinois named Barack Obama. After Obama was sworn in as president, Souza became the Chief Official White House Photographer. It is possible that Souza spent more time with the president than anyone except his family. In his tenure as White House photographer, Souza took more than 2 million pictures of Obama. Social media gave him the opportunity to show his work widely. "I happened to be the person in this job when all these social media tools came into existence," he said. "I mean, Instagram did not exist before this administration."

Today Souza has continued to post pictures of Obama's presidency on his Instagram account. His photographs have also appeared in exhibits around the U.S. Recently, his favorite photos of his time covering Obama were published in a best-selling book, *Obama: An Intimate Portrait*. Obama himself contributed the foreword to the book.

Others favored using a cruise missile strike to take him out during his daily walk in the garden. Ultimately, Obama decided to use SEAL Team Six to invade the compound. In the months leading up to the actual operation, the matter was discussed at length.

Two of the most important participants involved in those discussions were actually not in the room with the president when the famous picture was taken. Leon Panetta was managing the operation from CIA headquarters in Langley, Virginia, and William McRaven was in Afghanistan, close to his men. But Thomas Donilon, the deputy national security adviser, was there.

It was Donilon who had told Obama eight months earlier, in August 2010, that the guys at Langley thought they had something: the first credible evidence of bin Laden's whereabouts in eight years. The lead came through U.S. intelligence, which had tracked an al-Qaida operative named Abu Ahmed al-Kuwaiti to the compound outside of Abbottabad that would become the site of the raid. At that same August meeting, Panetta showed the president pictures and maps and made his case that the mysterious pacer might be bin Laden.

"This is the best lead that we have seen since Tora Bora [the last time bin Laden was seen]," one of the team members said. While intrigued, Obama was not sure the man was bin Laden. The photos intelligence

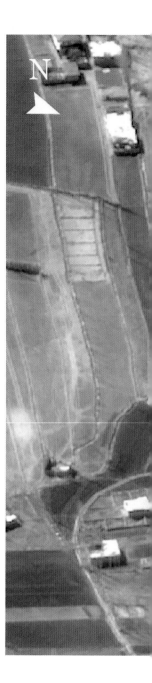

An aerial view of the Abbottabad compound with an inset of Pakistan. The left view shows the area before the compound was built.

operatives had gathered of the pacer were from indirect angles, making it difficult to see his face or even tell precisely how tall he was. Later, Obama recalled not being particularly hopeful because the pacer could have been anyone.

Even so, one major figure in the Obama administration, John Brennan, assistant to the president for counterterrorism, felt confident that they had their man. After years studying the infamous terrorist, Brennan thought he recognized bin Laden's specific way of walking. In any event, teams were set up to keep the compound under close watch.

So, the compound was watched for months. On December 14 Panetta visited the president again. Both men were struck by the fact that the family on the third floor of the compound never left the building. Obviously, they were hiding. But why? As always, Obama and his team were fascinated by photos of the pacer on his daily walks. Despite Brennan's intuition, there was still a chance that the mystery man could be anyone. Even so, Obama couldn't help but feel a little bit hopeful. He asked Panetta to start thinking about plans for action.

At first Panetta planned to use his own CIA teams to invade the compound. But after meeting with SEAL leader McRaven, he quickly realized that the Navy SEALs were uniquely qualified for the mission. Obama met with his national security team on March 14 to go over all the information. The most senior CIA analyst on the team put the odds that the pacer was bin Laden at 95 percent. But others weren't nearly as certain. Others put their level of confidence 80 percent and some as low as 40 or 30 percent.

THE TRAINING OF A NAVY SEAL

Navy SEALs go through rigorous training, including swimming in subzero temperatures.

Navy SEALs are some of the best-trained people in the U.S. military. Howard Wasdin is a veteran of SEAL Team Six, the squad that killed Osama bin Laden. After leaving the service, Wasdin wrote a memoir of his time in the SEALs, including a section on his training—a brutal process designed to separate true warriors from the rest of the pack. A Navy SEAL trainee is expected to run strenuously, negotiate difficult obstacle courses, and swim in the freezing cold ocean—and that's just the tip of the iceberg.

For instance, one of the drills trainees have to pass is called "drown-proofing." In this exercise, the trainee's hands are bound together, as are the feet. Then he has to hop into the deep end of a pool, bob up and down 20 times, float, swim to the shallow end of the pool (still bound!), turn without touching the bottom, swim back to the deep end, do a forward and backward somersault underwater, then retrieve a face mask from the bottom of the pool—with his teeth!

As Wasdin described it, the danger was constant.

He wrote, "The torment continued throughout each day—push-ups, runs, push-ups, calisthenics, push-ups, swims, push-ups, O-course—day after day, week after week. We ran a mile one-way just to eat a meal. Round-trip multiplied by three meals made for six miles a day just to eat! We never seemed to have enough time to recover. . . ."

The most feared part of the training was "Hell Week," which gets its name from the brutal training SEALs go through during that week. As one example, trainees swim icy waters in an effort to make them as cold and tired as physically possible. For those who survive Hell Week, more difficult training awaits, along with written tests on various pieces of military history and tactics.

How do Navy SEALs get through this rigorous training? In truth, many don't. But those who pass are the elite, just like the members of SEAL Team Six. SEAL Team Six was considered the best SEAL team in the U.S. military! The U.S. government needed to use the best if it had any chance of capturing bin Laden.

The CIA had become extremely cautious after making an enormous mistake during the Bush administration. In 2002 the CIA had mistakenly told the president that there were weapons of mass destruction in Iraq when there weren't any. This error led to a U.S.–led invasion of Iraq in 2003 and the deaths of hundreds of thousands of Iraqis and thousands of U.S. soldiers over the next eight years of the war.

In the end, despite the uncertainty, the president found himself agreeing with those who said they had their man. On April 7, 2011, McRaven's team of SEALs undertook their first rehearsal at Bagram Air Base in Afghanistan, where a copy of bin Laden's compound had been built for practice. The first run-throughs involved the actual raid of the compound. Other rehearsals tested the helicopters. After months of preparation, SEAL Team Six was ready. On April 28 a National Security Council meeting took place—it was time to make a final decision. Some of the same people in that meeting were also in the Situation Room for Pete Souza's famous photograph. Obama sat at the head of a conference room table. Around the table sat Vice President Joe Biden, Secretary of Defense Robert Gates, Secretary of State Hillary Clinton, Chairman of the Joint Chiefs of Staff Admiral Mike Mullen, General James Cartwright, Assistant to the President

CIA head Leon Panetta was one of the chief decision makers in the Situation Room.

for Homeland Security John Brennan, National Security Adviser Thomas Donilon, Director of National Intelligence James Clapper, CIA head Leon Panetta, and his deputy, Mike Morell.

As for Admiral McRaven, he was in Afghanistan,
waiting for the "go" order.

One by one, the team was asked to choose among
three options: bombing the compound, taking the
pacer out with a missile strike, or bringing in the
Navy SEALs. Nearly everyone voted for the raid.
Secretary of State Clinton favored a raid despite
the risk that it could strain relations with Pakistan.
Likewise, Brennan, Donilon, Clapper, and Morell all
voted to send in the SEALs.

Panetta put it like this, "What would the average

American say if he knew we had the best chance of getting bin Laden since Tora Bora and we didn't take a shot?"

The two major dissenters were Biden and Gates. Biden said it was too risky politically. After all, if the SEAL team went in and bin Laden wasn't there, Obama would not win a second term. As for Gates, he favored taking a shot at bin Laden from a drone, worried that a direct assault could go horribly wrong. U.S. troops could get killed. A helicopter could crash. However, the next day, at the urging of his two top

WILLIAM H. MCRAVEN

U.S. Navy Admiral William McRaven designed the plan for the raid on bin Laden's compound.

The undisputed heroes of Operation Neptune Spear were the members of SEAL Team Six and their leader, U.S. Navy Admiral William H. McRaven. Born on November 6, 1955, McRaven graduated from the University of Texas at Austin and became a Navy SEAL in 1978. By the time al-Qaida was an international terrorist organization, McRaven had been in command at practically every level in the field of special operations. When President Obama tapped him to formulate a strategy to kill Osama bin Laden, McRaven was the Commander of the Joint Special Operations Command. Quickly earning the trust of Obama and CIA Director Leon Panetta, McRaven designed the plan and trained the men who broke into bin Laden's compound.

His philosophy has since become part of the curriculum at the naval postgraduate school: a small, well-trained force can almost always take out a larger, well-defended foe. McRaven described the qualities needed to bring off such an action this way: "A simple plan, carefully concealed, realistically rehearsed, and executed with surprise, speed, and purpose."

During the last few years of his service, McRaven became a "Bull Frog," the name given the longest-serving Navy SEAL still on active duty. McRaven retired from the Navy on August 28, 2014, and is now chancellor of the University of Texas System, which consists of eight universities and six health institutions.

"It was a matter of taking one last breath. . . . We weren't going to have better certainty about whether bin Laden was there, and so it was just a matter of pulling the trigger."

aides, Gates changed his mind and told Obama that he favored sending in the SEALs.

President Obama had pretty much made up his mind by the end of the meeting. Even so, he stayed up late that night to think it over. "It was a matter of taking one last breath," Obama said, "and just making sure, asking is there something that I haven't thought of? . . . We weren't going to have better certainty about whether bin Laden was there, and so it was just a matter of pulling the trigger." In the end, McRaven's confidence coupled with his meticulous preparation and ability helped make Obama's decision easier. As the president put it, "McRaven, he inspires confidence."

ChapterFour
THE MIDDLE EAST AFTER BIN LADEN

Though killing bin Laden had great psychological and symbolic meaning for Americans, his death did not bring an end to terrorism. Most historians agree that Obama did a good job of rooting out al-Qaida. His decision to take out bin Laden was a brave risk that paid off. However, at the same time that Obama was aggressively using drones to kill al-Qaida leaders, he was also taking troops out of Iraq. As a result, there were fewer U.S. soldiers there to help defend the country. Without U.S. troops to block them, a new terrorist group arose: ISIS, or the Islamic State in Iraq and Syria.

Founded in 2004, ISIS got off to a slow start, fading from view in light of a U.S. surge, or influx, of troops in Iraq in 2006 and 2007. But as the U.S. dialed down its involvement in the region, ISIS (also called ISIL or Daesh) ramped up its activities. As Iraq and especially Syria became more and more unstable, ISIS occupied miles of land and unleashed a campaign of vicious murder against non-believers. In 2014 a series of video-streamed public beheadings of Western journalists shocked the world. On June 29, 2014, ISIS leader Abu Bakr al-Baghdadi announced a new country or "caliphate" that stretched over the lands they had occupied from Aleppo in Syria to Diyala in Iraq.

The U.S. airstrikes on Syria looked like a vast cloud of smoke from nearby Turkey.

Though Obama was aggressive from day one in his response to bin Laden and al-Qaida, he was slower to recognize the ISIS threat. But once Obama acted, he did so forcefully. On August 7, 2014, a U.S.–led coalition began airstrikes against ISIS in Iraq. On October 15 the U.S. launched Operation Inherent Resolve, a military offensive that, as of August 2017, had led to almost 25,000 airstrikes on Iraq and Syria. Driven into retreat, ISIS has been weakened. Even so, it has not been destroyed—far from it. Today, ISIS remains a terrorist organization capable of engineering major attacks. In October 2015, ISIS claimed to have bombed a Russian airplane, killing 224 people. On November 13, 2015,

ISIS gunmen and suicide bombers killed 130 people
in Paris, France. Two years later, on November 24,
2017, ISIS took credit for bombing a mosque in Egypt
that killed more than 300 people. They have taken
credit for numerous attacks around the world.

But terrorism tells only part of the story of the
Middle East. After years of mistreatment by their
mostly totalitarian governments, citizens in many
countries across the region have demanded equal

rights. This movement, known as "the Arab Spring," peaked at the very beginning of 2011, the same year that the United States killed bin Laden. Many historians point to an event in the African country of Tunisia as the start of these protests that echoed throughout the Arab world.

It began simply. Mohammed Bouazizi was a 26-year-old fruit vendor and the sole breadwinner for a family of seven. But his cart wasn't licensed so he couldn't legally sell his wares. As a result, on December 17, 2010, a policewoman seized his cart. He tried to pay the standard fine so he could get his cart back, but she refused to accept the money or return the cart. Instead, she spat in his face and insulted his dead father. Furious and humiliated, Bouazizi marched to a government building and tried to talk to government officials. When they refused to take his complaint seriously, Bouazizi set himself on fire. He died on January 4, 2011. With the help of the Internet and social media, the gruesome footage spread around Tunisia almost instantly. Soon, violent protests began in the streets. Protesters in one town set fire to police cars and even a police station. Police fired back, killing a teenage protester. Across the country, dozens of protesters were killed.

On January 14, Tunisian President Zine el Abidine Ben Ali fled into exile. While Obama and McRaven were planning the attack on bin Laden, the people

Thousands gathered in Tunisia to demonstrate in favor of freedom of the press.

of Tunisia were building a new government. A democratic election for a new Constituent Assembly, the governing body of Tunisia, was held on October 23, 2011.

Other countries followed Tunisia's lead to gain greater freedom for their citizens. Following a wave of protests in Egypt, President Hosni Mubarak stepped down on February 11, 2011. Then on February 15, antigovernment protests began in Libya, leading to a war between rebels and the government forces of Colonel Muammar Gaddafi, one of the Middle East's most infamous dictators. Ultimately, the government was overthrown on August 23 of that year. Gaddafi was killed on October 20. Protests also took place in Algeria, Bahrain, United Arab Emirates, Jordan, Syria, Saudi Arabia, Yemen, Morocco, and Oman.

The Arab Spring and the spread of democracy were cheered on by President Obama and other Western leaders. Even so, not every protest in every country led to a positive change. Syria, in particular, was spun into a horrific civil war that rages to this day—a tragedy that has left close to half a million Syrians dead and has forced 12 million people, half of the country's prewar population, from their homes.

How did such a nightmare begin? Some historians point to global warming as one of the causes. Global warming brings extremes of weather. A drought that lasted from 2006 to 2010 caused a million and a half people to migrate to already crowded cities. Unfortunately, as economic conditions worsened, Syrian President Bashar al-Assad did very little to

The war in Syria meant that many, many people lost their homes and were forced to flee to other countries.

respond to citizen's pleas for help. A tense situation turned bloody in March 2011 when 23 boys were arrested and then tortured for writing graffiti in support of the Arab Spring. As anger grew, al-Assad's troops imprisoned and killed protesters. The country picked sides. During the summer of 2011, ex-Syrian military formed the Free Syrian Army to overthrow the government. Civil war followed and has raged ever since, leading to a refugee crisis that has spread across Europe.

THE SYRIAN CIVIL WAR

Members of the Free Syrian Army ready themselves for battle.

As Syria has continued to be involved in a civil war, more than a dozen countries have gotten involved. They are: Russia, Great Britain, France, the U.S., Australia, Iran, Saudi Arabia, Qatar, UAE, Lebanon, Jordan, Turkey, Iraq, and Israel.

The primary pro-government organizations and countries are:

- Bashar Al-Assad, the Syrian dictator, and his followers
- Iran
- Hezbollah, a Shiite militia and terrorist organization
- Russia, a longstanding friend of Syria

The antigovernment forces are:

- the Free Syrian Army (FSA)
- the Kurds (an ethnic minority across Syria, Turkey, Iraq, and Iran)
- Saudi Arabia
- Turkey
- the United States

Terror groups have also joined the fighting against Assad's government. They are ISIS, a group born out of al-Qaida in Iraq, and the Al Nusra Front, a group born out of al-Qaida in Syria.

With so many countries and groups fighting or supplying weapons, it is hard to know how or when the war will end. Even if Assad falls, there is no stable unified opposition ready to replace him. In fact, Assad's defeat would likely lead to even more fighting over who the new ruler will be. On the other hand, if Assad ultimately wins the war, it would likely be at the cost of years of death and suffering. A negotiated truce would be the best option. But with so many different groups fighting, getting everyone to agree on a single solution will be difficult.

Former President Obama continues to speak for U.S. values in the face of tyranny.

Indeed, as the world community looks to the future, containing ISIS and Islamic extremism remains a major challenge. But it is a challenge that the United States and its allies are trying to face. President Donald Trump has followed Obama's lead in keeping strong military pressure on ISIS in Iraq and Syria as well as the rest of the region, including Pakistan and Afghanistan. Hopefully, over time, ISIS will be weakened to the point where it is no longer a serious threat.

President Obama congratulates Admiral McRaven on the success of the bin Laden raid.

Regardless of the outcome of the continuing fight against ISIS, Obama deserves significant credit for helping to bring down al-Qaida. The planning of bin Laden's killing stands as one of the finest hours of his presidency. Admiral McRaven and SEAL Team Six responded to the challenge with poise and courage. The members of the Obama administration, who were captured by Pete Souza on camera as they awaited the outcome of that fateful raid—are now part of U.S. history. As the saying goes, a picture can be worth a thousand words. Souza's photo captured the notion of American will for the Obama years, just as the famous images of marines raising the flag at Iwo Jima during World War II and George Washington crossing the Delaware during the Revolutionary War did for their respective eras. Indeed, as generations pass, the United States has remained a country that doesn't look for conflict but is never afraid to act decisively to protect its values.

WHERE ARE THEY NOW?

Hillary Clinton continues to speak for progressive values and equal rights for women.

After the raid on bin Laden's compound, many of those involved continued in the Obama administration. Today, those who were there are serving the country in different ways.

Joe Biden teaches at the University of Pennsylvania.

Barack Obama is working on new ways to get young people involved in politics.

Marshall B. Webb is a lieutenant general and commander in the U.S. Air Force Special Operations Command (AFSOC).

Mike Mullen is a retired U.S. Navy Admiral and a visiting professor at the Woodrow Wilson School of Public and International Affairs at Princeton University.

Thomas Donilon works at the law firm O'Melveny & Myers. He has served as chair of the Commission on Enhancing National Cybersecurity since April 13, 2016.

Bill Daley ran for governor of Illinois in 2013, then joined Argentiere Capital as a managing partner.

Denis McDonough joined the Markle Foundation, a group dedicated to boosting job opportunities for U.S. citizens.

Tony Blinken finished the Obama presidency as deputy secretary of state.

Hillary Clinton ran for president in 2016. She founded "Onward Together," an organization that works to promote progressive values. She also writes and lectures around the country.

Audrey Tomason's activities are unknown.

John Brennan served from 2013 through the end of Obama's presidency as the head of the CIA. He is now a senior adviser of the University of Texas' Intelligence Studies Project.

James Clapper joined the Center for a New American Security (CNAS), a Washington, D.C.–based think tank, as a Distinguished Senior Fellow for Intelligence and National Security.

Robert Gates was the president of the Boy Scouts of America and chancellor of William and Mary.

Timeline

1957

Osama bin Laden is born

1979

The Soviet Union invades Afghanistan

1990

Saddam Hussein, ruler of Iraq, invades Kuwait

1996

Osama bin Laden declares war on the United States

1980

U.S. attempt to rescue hostages held in Iran fails when a helicopter crashes

1987

Osama bin Laden forms a fighting troop in Afghanistan

2000

al-Qaida attacks the warship USS *Cole*

September 11, 2001

Hijacked planes smash into the World Trade Center in New York City, the Pentagon in Washington, D.C., and Shanksville, Penn., killing almost 3,000 people

Timeline

2003

The United States invades Iraq

November 2008

Barack Obama is elected president

May 1, 2011

Obama speaks at
the White House
Correspondents' Dinner

May 2, 2011

Osama bin Laden is killed in a
SEAL Team Six raid

May 2009

Obama tells his team that he wants the hunt for bin Laden to "come to the front of the line"

December 2010

The "pacer" at the compound is identified as possibly being bin Laden

2011

The Arab Spring and the Syrian civil war begin

2013

ISIS steps up global terrorism, including killing journalists on video

Glossary

affiliated—officially connected or attached to another organization

anti-Semitism—discrimination against Jews, because of their cultural background, religion, or race

compromise—a settlement in which each side gives up part of its demands and agrees to the final product

courier— a person who delivers important messages

devout—deeply devoted to one's religion

dissenter—a person who refuses to accept the teachings or rules of an official state church or political institution

freelance—to earn a living independently; a freelancer is paid for individual jobs by different companies

implicate—to show to be connected or involved, usually in a crime

infidel—a person who does not believe in a particular religion, or any religion

meticulous—to show great attention to detail

mujahideen—guerrilla fighters in Islamic countries, fighting against non-Muslim forces

notorious—being well-known for something bad

roast—to criticize severely in a joking way

scour—to search a place thoroughly

secular—not controlled by a religious body or concerned with religious matters

sovereignty—a supreme power, usually over a politically organized unit

totalitarian—a political system in which the government has complete control over its people

Additional Resources

Further Reading

Gormley, Beatrice. *Barack Obama: Our Forty-Fourth President*. New York: Simon & Schuster, 2015.

January, Brendan. *ISIS: The Global Face of Terrorism*. Minneapolis, Minn.: Lerner Publishing, 2018.

Zullo, Allan. *10 True Tales: Heroes of 9/11*. New York: Scholastic, 2015.

Internet Sites

Use FactHound to find Internet sites related to this book.
Visit *www.facthound.com*
Just type in 9780756558796 and go.

Critical Thinking Questions

If you were President Obama, would you have ordered the attack on bin Laden's compound? Why or why not?

Who do you think were the true heroes of Operation Neptune Spear? The Navy SEALs for executing the plan? William McRaven for training the troops? President Obama for approving the operation? Someone else? Support your answer.

How do you feel about photographers being allowed to follow presidents around the White House at all times? Do you think it compromises national security? Support your answer.

Source Notes

p. 5, "You, you, you, and you…" Mark Bowden. *The Finish, The Killing of Osama Bin Laden.* New York: Grove Press, 2012, p. 58.

p. 5, "Here's the Deal…" Ibid., p. 59.

p. 9, "Godspeed to you and your forces…" Ibid., p. 212.

p. 12, "Go in there…" Ibid., p. 220.

p. 13, "I need to watch this…" Nicholas Schmidle. "Getting Bin Laden." *The New Yorker*, August 8, 2011, p. 15.

p. 15, "Mr. Director, as you can see…" *The Finish, The Killing of Osama Bin Laden*, p. 226.

p. 16, "For God and country…" Ibid., p. 230.

p. 18, "I have fairly high confidence…" Ibid., p. 234.

p. 18, "Tonight, I can report to the…" Ibid., p. 235.

p. 19, "I want to meet that dog…" "Getting Bin Laden," p. 28.

p. 21, "Islam is a system given by God…" *The Finish, The Killing of Osama Bin Laden*, p. 33.

p. 22, "God willing, we want the Lion's Den…" Ibid., p. 38.

p. 25, "He hunches forth…" Ibid., p. 42.

p. 26, "I'm declaring war on the United States…" Ibid., p. 45.

p. 30, "I don't think there's really anyone else in the White House…" Mike Hoffman and Alex Reside. "Pete Souza on Making Pictures for History." *GQ Magazine*, January 2017.

p. 30, "I see all the different compartments of his life…" Ibid.

p. 34, "This is the best lead that we have seen…" Mark Bowden. "Hunt for Geronimo." *Vanity Fair*, Oct. 12, 2012, p. 5.

p. 37, "the torment continued…" Howard E. Wasdin and Stephen Templin. "A Veteran of Seal Team Six Describes His Training." *Vanity Fair*, May 4, 2011.

p. 42, "A simple plan, carefully concealed…" Ibid., p. 149.

cxdqwp. 43, "It was a matter of taking one last breath…" Ibid., p. 16.

p. 43, "McRaven—he inspires confidence…" *The Finish, The Killing of Osama Bin Laden*, p. 45.

Select Bibliography

Bacevich, Andrew J. *America's War for the Greater Middle East: a Military History*. New York: Random House, 2017.

Bowden, Mark. *The Finish, The Killing of Osama Bin Laden*. New York: Grove Press, 2012.

O'Neill, Robert. *The Operator, Firing the Shots That Killed Osama Bin Laden*. New York: Scribner's, 2017.

Index

Afghanistan, 4, 9, 11, 12, 18, 22–23, 24, 25, 28, 29, 34, 38, 40, 52, 56, 57
Ahmed, Abrar, 15
Ahmed, Bushra, 15
al-Kuwaiti, Abu Ahmed, 34
al-Qaida, 9, 26, 42
    terrorist group, 4, 18, 24, 28, 29, 34, 44, 51, 53, 57
announcement, 18
Arab Spring, 47–49, 50, 59
al-Assad, Bashar, 49–50, 51
attack options, 7–9, 34, 40–41, 41, 43

al-Baghdadi, Abu Bakr, 44
Ben Ali, Zine el Abidine, 47
Biden, Joe, 17, 38, 41, 55
bin Laden, Osama, 5, 25, 32, 34, 36, 41
bin Laden, Khalid, 15
bin Laden, Mohammed bin Awad, 20
bin Laden, Osama, 4, 6, 7–8, 11, 15–16, 18, 20, 22–24, 26, 28, 29, 44, 53, 56, 57, 58, 59
Blinken, Tony, 17, 55
Bouazizi, Mohammed, 47
Brennan, John O., 17, 36, 39, 40, 55
Bush, George H.W., 24
Bush, George W., 4, 29, 38

Cairo (dog), 19
Carter, Jimmy, 32
Cartwright, James, 38
CIA, 4, 6, 11, 34, 36, 38, 39, 55
civil war, 49, 50, 51, 59
Clapper, James R., Jr., 17, 39, 40, 55
Clinton, Bill, 4, 26
Clinton, Hillary Rodham, 13, 17, 38, 40, 55
crisis, 50

Daley, Bill, 17, 55
Donilon, Thomas E., 4–5, 17, 34, 39, 40, 55
drones, 8, 41, 44

Egypt, 46, 49
Emanuel, Rahm, 4–5

Fahd, king of Saudi Arabia, 24

Gaddafi, Muammar, 49
Gates, Robert M., 17, 38, 41, 43, 55
global warming, 49

helicopters, 9, 12–13, 15, 38, 41, 57
Hussein, Saddam, 24, 56

identification, 6, 7–8, 18, 32, 34–36, 36, 59
Iran, 32, 51, 57
Iraq, 24, 29, 38, 44, 45, 51, 52, 56, 58
ISIS, 44–46, 51, 52, 59
Islamic religion, 20, 21–22, 24, 52

Kuwait, 24, 56

Leiter, Mike, 4–5
Leutze, Emanuael Gottlieb, 17
Libya, 49
Lion's Den, 22

McDonough, Denis, 17, 55
McRaven, William H., 9, 11, 15, 16, 18, 34, 36, 38, 40, 42, 43, 53
Miller, John, 26
Morell, Mike, 39, 40
Mubarak, Hosni, 49
mujahideen, 22, 25
Mullen, Michael, 17, 38, 55

Navy SEALs, 9, 12, 15, 16, 18, 19, 32, 34, 36, 37, 38, 40, 41, 42, 43, 53, 58

Obama, Barack, 4–5, 6, 7–8, 9, 11, 13, 15, 16, 17, 18, 19, 29, 30, 32, 33, 34, 35, 36, 38, 41, 42, 43, 44, 45, 49, 52, 53, 55, 58, 59
Operation Inherent Resolve, 45

Pakistan, 6, 7, 8, 9, 12, 40, 52
Panetta, Leon, 4–5, 11, 12, 15, 34, 36, 39, 40–41, 42

Qutb, Sayyid, 20–22

Reagan, Ronald, 32, 33
rehearsals, 38, 42

Saudi Arabia, 20, 24, 26, 49, 51
September 11 attacks, 4, 28–29, 57
Souza, Pete, 15, 30, 32, 33, 38, 53–54
Soviet Union, 22, 24, 56
Syria, 20, 22, 44, 45, 49–50, 51, 52, 59

Taliban, 29
Tomason, Audrey, 17, 55
Trump, Donald, 52
Tunisia, 47–48, 49

United States, 7, 24, 25, 26, 51, 54, 56, 58
USS Cole, 26, 57

video feed, 11–12, 13

Wasdin, Howard, 37
Washington, George, 17, 54
Webb, Marshall B., 17, 55
White House Correspondents' Dinner, 11, 58
World Trade Center, 4, 26, 29, 57

About the Author

Dan Elish has written numerous works of nonfiction for young readers. He is also the author of 10 novels, including the upcoming *The Royal Order of Fighting Dragons*. He lives in New York City.